Sor for Guitar

35 Easy to Intermediate Original Works for Guitar
35 leichte bis mittelschwere Originalwerke für Gitarre
by / von
Fernando Sor (1778–1839)

Edited by / Herausgegeben von
Martin Hegel

ED 22349
ISMN 979-0-001-15909-8

www.schott-music.com

Mainz · London · Berlin · Madrid · New York · Paris · Prague · Tokyo · Toronto
© 2015 SCHOTT MUSIC GmbH & Co. KG, Mainz · Printed in Germany

Vorwort

Fernando Sor, geboren am 14. Februar 1778 in Barcelona, gestorben am 10. Juli 1839 in Paris, zählt zu den herausragenden Persönlichkeiten in der Geschichte der Gitarre, vor allem des frühen 19. Jahrhunderts. Schon zu seiner Zeit war er neben Giuliani, Aguado und Carulli nicht nur einer der führenden Gitarristen, sondern auch ein begnadeter Pädagoge und ein vielfältiger, genialer Komponist für sein Instrument. Nicht selten als „Schubert" oder auch „Beethoven der Gitarre" bezeichnet, war ihm das plumpe Virtuosentum eher fremd.

Sor schaffte es wie kein Zweiter, den mehrstimmigen klassischen bzw. frühromantischen Satz auf die Gitarre zu übertragen und setzte somit in seinen Werken neue Maßstäbe. Diese Tatsache wurde vor allem ermöglicht durch die entscheidenden Neuerungen in der Bauweise der Gitarre (sechs einfache Saiten, erhöhtes Griffbrett etc.), die der sogenannten „Blütezeit der Gitarre" den Weg ebneten. Nicht zuletzt seine musikalische Ausbildung, die er u.a. im spanischen Kloster Montserrat genoss, machte ihn zu einem begnadeten Komponisten, der die Gitarrenmusik durch eine anspruchsvolle und ausgefeilte Satztechnik bereicherte.

Seinen zupfenden Zeitgenossen war Sors Musik teilweise zu sperrig, zu anstrengend und zu schwierig. Man warf ihm sogar vor, er würde „gegen" die Gitarre komponieren. Seine Musik ist aber sehr genau für die Gitarre entworfen, Sor war nur im Gegensatz zu seinen Komponistenkollegen nicht immer kompromissbereit, was die Rücksichtnahme auf spieltechnische Belange betrifft. Nicht zuletzt aus diesem Grund zählt er zu den wichtigsten Gitarrenkomponisten. Seine Werke sind eine Bereicherung für das Repertoire unseres Instruments: Sor for Guitar!

Die vorliegende Sammlung will einen Einstieg in Fernando Sors Œuvre ermöglichen und enthält die leichtesten seiner Kompositionen, angefangen von kleinen Etüden und Übungsstücken bis hin zu leichteren Vortrags- und Konzertstücken. Glücklicherweise hat Sor durch seine Lehrtätigkeit (letztlich auch aus Geldmangel) eine Vielzahl kleiner, dankbarer Übungsstücke komponiert. Diese sind für den Anfänger konzipiert und auch heute noch hervorragend für den Unterricht geeignet. Sie sind entzückend und von besonderer Schönheit und es ist erstaunlich, wie einfallsreich Sor diese kleinen Stücke technisch wie musikalisch gestaltet hat.

Die meisten Fingersätze stammen original von Sor, nur selten hat der Herausgeber behutsame Modernisierungen vorgenommen und Fingersätze ergänzt. Alle Verzierungen und Bindungen werden originalgetreu wiedergegeben, können aber als optional betrachtet werden.

Martin Hegel

Preface

Fernando Sor, who was born in Barcelona on 14 February 1778 and died in Paris on 10 July 1839, is one of the most prominent figures in the history of the guitar, particularly from the early nineteenth Century. During his lifetime he was not only one of the leading guitarists alongside Giuliani, Aguado and Carulli, but also a gifted teacher and a brilliant and versatile composer for his instrument. Quite often referred to as a Schubert or Beethoven of the guitar, he did not tend to indulge in mere virtuoso display.

Sor succeeded better than any other in interpreting the polyphonic Classical and early Romantic style on the guitar, setting new standards in the quality of his music. This was made possible above all by important innovations in the construction of the guitar (six simple strings, raised fingerboard etc.) that prepared the way for what would be known as the heyday of that instrument. His musical training, some of it acquired at the Spanish monastery of Montserrat, served to make him a gifted composer who enriched the guitar repertoire with his demanding and refined musical technique.

Sor's music was sometimes too cumbersome, too demanding and too difficult for guitarists among his contemporaries, some of whom accused him of composing in conflict with the instrument. His music is however very precisely designed for the guitar, while unlike his fellow composers, Sor was not always ready to compromise and make concessions with regard to technical demands. It is also for this reason that he ranks among the most important composers of guitar music. His works are valuable additions to the repertoire of our instrument: Sor for guitar!

This collection aims to offer an introduction to Fernando Sor's oeuvre and contains the easiest of his compositions, starting with little studies and exercises and extending to his easier recital and concert pieces. Sor fortunately composed numerous rewarding little exercises for use in his teaching (necessary to supplement his meagre income). These are designed for beginners and still eminently suitable for tuition purposes to this day. They are charming and particularly lovely: from a technical and musical point of view, Sor was astonishingly imaginative in crafting these little pieces.

Most of the fingerings originate from Sor himself, though occasionally the editor has suggested modern alternatives and marked in additional fingerings. All the ornaments and slurs are reproduced as in the original, though they may be regarded as optional.

Martin Hegel
Translation Julia Rushworth

Inhalt / Contents

3 Etüden / 3 Studies, aus / from op. 31 *(Leçons progressives)*
Leçon No. 1 5
Leçon No. 2 6
Leçon No. 3 7

10 Etüden / 10 Studies, aus / from op. 60 *(Introduction à l´ étude de la guitare)*
Leçon No. 1 8
Leçon No. 2 8
Leçon No. 3 9
Leçon No. 4 9
Leçon No. 5 10
Leçon No. 6 11
Leçon No. 10 12
Leçon No. 13 12
Leçon No. 14 13
Leçon No. 19 13

7 Stücke / 7 Pieces, aus / from op. 44 *(Petites pièces progressives)*
No. 1 14
No. 2 14
No. 3 15
No. 6 16
No. 9 16
No. 11 17
No. 14 17

5 Etüden / 5 Studies, aus / from op. 35 *(24 Exercices très faciles)*
No. 1 18
No. 2 18
No. 3 19
No. 4 20
No. 14 21

Valse op. 51/1 22
Petite pièce facile op. 45/1 23
Marche op. 48/1 24
Divertissement op. 2/1 25
Theme et variations op. 45/3 25

5 mittelschwere Etüden / 5 Studies in medium difficulty
1 op. 35/17 28
2 op. 35/22 30
3 op. 31/23 32
4 op. 35/13 33
5 op. 6/1 34

3 Etüden / 3 Studies
aus / from op. 31
(« Leçons progressives »)
Leçon No. 1

Fernando Sor
1778-1839

Andante

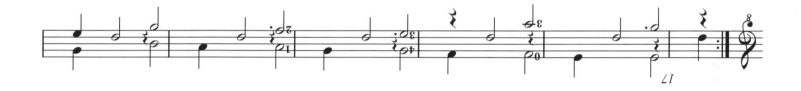

© 2015 Schott Music GmbH & Co. KG, Mainz

Leçon No. 2

Andante

Leçon No. 3

Allegretto moderato

10 Etüden / 10 Studies
aus / from op. 60
(« Introduction à l' étude de la guitare »)
Leçon No. 1

Fernando Sor

Leçon No. 2

Leçon No. 3

Leçon No. 4

Leçon No. 5

Leçon No. 6

D.C. al Fine

Fine

12

Leçon No. 10

Leçon No. 13

Leçon No. 14

Andante

Leçon No. 19

Fine

D.C. al Fine

7 Stücke / 7 Pieces
aus / from op. 44
(«Petites Pièces Progressives»)
No. 1

Fernando Sor

No. 2

No. 3

Andantino

15

16

No. 6

Moderato

© 2015 Schott Music GmbH & Co. KG, Mainz

No. 9

Andantino

© 2015 Schott Music GmbH & Co. KG, Mainz

Tempo di minuetto moderato

No. 14

Andante

No. 11

5 Etüden / 5 Studies
aus / from op. 35
(« 24 Exercices très faciles »)
No. 1

Fernando Sor

No. 2

No. 3

Larghetto

No. 4

No. 14

Andante

Valse
op. 51/1

Fernando Sor

Petite pièce facile
op. 45/1

Fernando Sor

Marche
op. 48/1

Fernando Sor

Divertissement
op. 2/1

Fernando Sor

Tempo di Minuetto

Thème et variations
op. 45/3

Fernando Sor

Andante

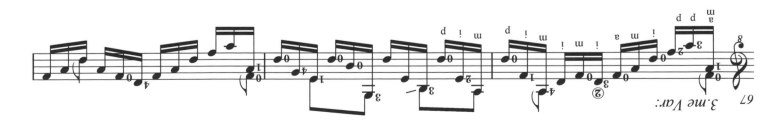

3.me Var:

5 mittelschwere Etüden
/ 5 Studies in medium difficulty

I. Etüde op. 35/17

Fernando Sor

II. Étude op. 35/22

Allegretto

III. Étude op. 31/23

Mouvement de prière religieuse

IV. Etüde op. 35/13

V. Etüde op. 6/1

Allegro moderato

Gitarrenduette aus dem 18. und 19. Jahrhundert
Guitar duets from the 18th and 19th century
Duo de guitars des XVIIIe et XIXe siècles

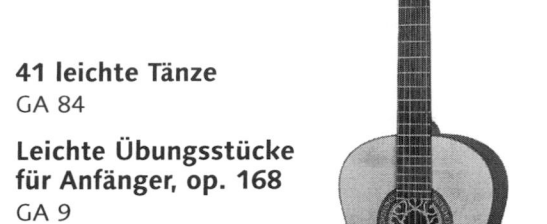

Ernst Gottlieb Baron
Sonate
GA 490

Ludwig van Beethoven
Sonatine d-Moll
nach der Sonatine c-Moll WoO 43/1
GA 439

Leonhard von Call
6 Duette, op. 24
GA 56

Leonhard von Call / T. Gaude
Serenade op. 39 / 6 Walzer
GA 39

Ferdinando Carulli
12 Duos
ED 5660

Zwei Duos, op. 146
ED 6014

Sechs kleine Duette, op. 34
Vol. 1 · GA 65, Nr. 1-3
Vol. 2 · GA 66, Nr. 4-6

Romanzen, op. 333/2
GA 68

Leichte fortschreitende Stücke,
op. 120
GA 87

Napoléon Coste
Barcarolle und Walzer
aus op. 51
GA 378

Claude Debussy
Danse bohémienne
GA 460

Children's Corner
GA 491

3 Préludes
GA 522

Duo-Schatzkiste
Originalwerke von der Barockzeit
bis zur Moderne
Hg. von Martin Hegel
ED 21383

Joseph Haydn
Duett in G
nach dem Original Hob. XII: 4
GA 449

Joseph Küffner
Zwölf Duette, op. 87
GA 45

Leichte Sonatinen, op. 80
GA 8

Leichte Duette
GA 83

41 leichte Tänze
GA 84

Leichte Übungsstücke
für Anfänger, op. 168
GA 9

Felix Mendelssohn
5 Lieder ohne Worte
GA 461

Giacomo Merchi
Vier Duette, op. 3
GA 470

Pietro Domenico Paradies
Sonata VIII
GA 516

Robert Schumann
14 Leichte Stücke
aus „Album für die Jugend", op. 68
GA 18

Fernando Sor
Leichte Duette für Anfänger
GA 389

Silvius Leopold Weiss
Duett
GA 454

SCHOTT
www.schott-music.com

R 3016-2 · 6-2012